RUTH GALLOWAY'S *norfolk*

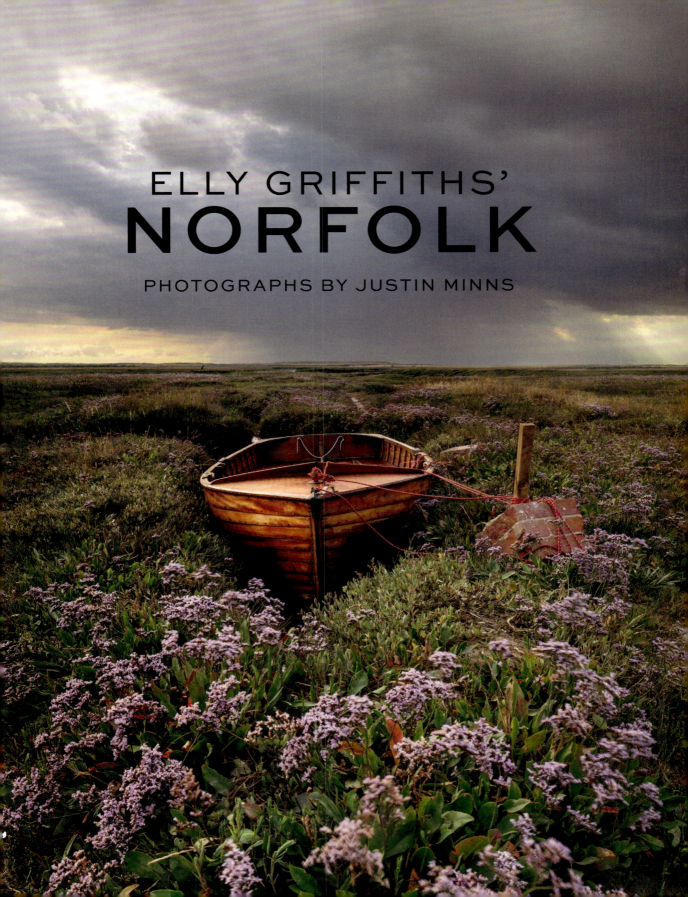

ELLY GRIFFITHS'
NORFOLK

PHOTOGRAPHS BY JUSTIN MINNS

ELLY GRIFFITHS'
NORFOLK

PHOTOGRAPHS BY JUSTIN MINNS

QUERCUS

CONTENTS

INTRODUCTION

In *The Crossing Places,* the first book to feature forensic archaeologist Dr Ruth Galloway, Ruth says she has no idea why she loves Norfolk. Unlike my fictional creation, I do have some idea why the place has such a hold on me. For a start, it has fond childhood associations. My grandmother and aunt both lived in Norfolk and I have very happy memories of drifting along the Broads in Aunt Marge's boat while she told stories of will-o'-the-wisps, ghostly apparitions and a spectral hound called Black Shuck. Folk memory is strong in East Anglia, perhaps because the area has been occupied for so long. The oldest human footprints outside Africa were found in Norfolk and people have been treading on the county's soil ever since. The archaeology, folklore and history make the most easterly part of England a gift for any novelist, particularly a crime writer.

Readers sometimes say that Norfolk is a character in my books. I think that's probably true and, like all good protagonists, it has many different facets, changing with the seasons and with the light, always offering new perspectives. This book is an attempt to explain just why Ruth and I love Norfolk so much.

SPRING

SPRING

'll never forget when I first met Ruth Galloway. I was walking across Titchwell Marsh, on the north Norfolk coast, with my husband, Andy, and our children, twins Alex and Juliet, then aged seven. We'd been staying with my Aunt Marjorie, who lived in Norwich, and Marge had suggested Titchwell as a bracing walk with a sandy beach at the end. Titchwell, just over an hour's drive from Norwich, is a nature reserve with fascinating habitats that include reedbeds, saltmarsh and freshwater lagoons where flocks of birds swoop and gather. But it was a cold spring day and all the wildlife seemed to be hiding. The marshes, so beautiful at sunrise and sunset, were grey and featureless. The flat landscape meant that you couldn't see the beach or even the sea. The children had begun to doubt its very existence.

Andy had recently left his City job to retrain as an archaeologist. Now, to fill the slightly grumpy silence, he started to tell us about the significance of the landscape.

'Prehistoric people thought that marshland was sacred. Because it's neither land nor sea, they saw it as a bridge to the afterlife. A sort of in-between place. That's why you find bodies buried there. You know, bog bodies. It's to mark that boundary between life and death.'

Right:
The Norfolk Marshes. Neither land nor sea, neither life nor death...

Left and above:
Ruth loves the marshes, their hidden
paths and secret inlets.

It's no exaggeration to say that the entire plot of *The
Crossing Places* came to me in that instant.

And I saw Dr Ruth Galloway walking towards me.

I knew her immediately. She was about forty, with
shoulder-length brown hair and a determined expression.
'Follow the feet', I tell my creative writing students. Ruth
was wearing walking shoes, spattered with mud and
sand. I followed her all the way back to the (imaginary)
University of North Norfolk, where she was a lecturer
in forensic archaeology. As Ruth climbs the steps to her
office, she sees a stranger waiting by the door. He looks
somehow ominous; too big, too serious, too *grown-up* to be
a mature student or even a lecturer.

Ruth's boss, Phil, is buzzing with news, 'This is
Detective Chief Inspector Harry Nelson. He wants to talk
to you about a murder.'

I didn't know then that this would be the start of fifteen books, that Ruth's adventures would eventually be read all round the world, that the books would win prizes and become bestsellers. I just knew that I had the idea for a story about a forensic archaeologist who lives in a beautiful, but rather isolated location on the north Norfolk coast. Ruth is asked to help the police when a child's bones are found on the marshes. The officer in charge, DCI Harry Nelson, wonders if they are the remains of a girl who went missing ten years ago. Ruth knows immediately that the bones are actually over two thousand years old but she is drawn into the case. And into a very complicated relationship with DCI Nelson.

That book was *The Crossing Places*. It was my first crime novel, although I had previously published four books under my own name, Domenica de Rosa. After reading the manuscript, my agent told me 'you need a crime name.' Without thinking too much about it, I chose Ellen Griffiths, which had been my grandmother's name. I didn't know her too well, she died when I was five, but I had always been told that she was a very clever woman who loved reading but had to leave school at thirteen to go into service. I thought she'd like to have her name on a book.

I also needed a new publisher. My previous publishers told me, very nicely, that they weren't interested in the new venture. Luckily my agent thought to send the manuscript to Quercus Books where it was acquired by a wonderful editor called Jane Wood. Jane saw something that she liked in Ruth – and in me – and, with her help, I got *The Crossing*

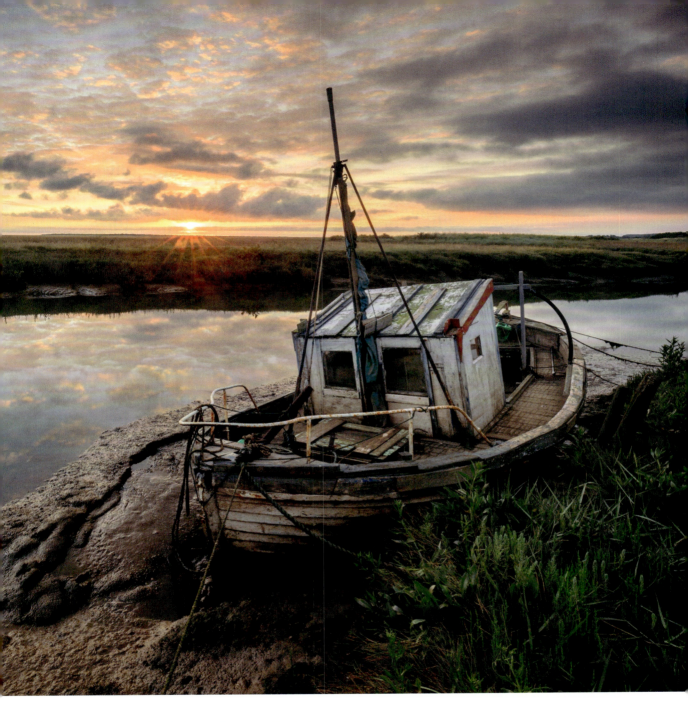

Places into publishable shape. Jane has edited all the Ruth books, which is very unusual in today's publishing world. Ruth and I are so lucky to have her.

Postscript: neither Jane or I can remember how Ellen became Elly. Perhaps it just looked tidier on the cover…

Following pages:

In prehistoric times, the Norfolk coast would have been covered by woodland.

Ruth's cottage is one of three, facing out across the marsh. It's loosely inspired by a line of cottages I first saw from the car park of Briarfields Hotel in Titchwell (where the women priests go to drink cocktails in *The Woman in Blue*). Ruth's neighbours have changed over the fifteen books but the view remains the same. Here it is, from *The Crossing Places*.

> 'Beyond her front garden with its windblown grass and broken blue fence there is nothingness. Just miles and miles of marshland, spotted with stunted gorse bushes and criss-crossed with small, treacherous streams. Everything is pale and washed out, grey-green merging to grey-white as the marsh meets the sky. Far off is the sea, a line of darker grey, seagulls riding in on the waves. It is utterly desolate and Ruth has absolutely no idea why she loves it so much.'

At first, I tried to keep the location of Ruth's cottage deliberately vague. I gave the area the generic name of 'the Saltmarsh' and placed her fictional university just outside King's Lynn. I thought that locals might not like to find dead bodies on their doorstep. That was before I knew Norfolk people well. After a few book tours, it became apparent that they loved fictional murders on

King's Lynn.
The town, once an important port, is central to the books. Nelson's police station is here and, in *The Crossing Places*, Ruth and Nelson have a meal by the quay.

their doorsteps and, as the books went on, I began to use real place names. Sometimes the locations are slightly fictionalized. Moulton Sea's End that features in *The House at Sea's End* is a version of Happisburgh. Blackstock Hall from *The Ghost Fields* owes a lot to Wiveton Hall. But Hunstanton, Wells, other areas of marshland such as Blakeney and Cley, then Cromer, King's Lynn, Norwich, Tombland and Grime's Graves all appear under their real names, as faithfully recreated as I can make them.

Above:
Cromer pier.

Opposite:
Windmill at Cley.

Following pages:
Hunstanton.

Right:
Norfolk bluebells.

The 'Saltmarsh' features in all the Ruth books. In *The Crossing Places*, Nelson receives sinister letters telling him to look for a missing child 'where the earth meets the sky.' The letters are full of religious symbolism but also contain references to Norse legend as well as archaeology. Here's a taste:

> 'Beware the water spirits and light bonfires on the beach. Beware the wicker man. Now the sun turns southwards and evil spirts walk abroad. Follow the will o'the wisps, the spirits of dead children. Who knows where they will lead you?'

These references cause Nelson to suspect Cathbad, a local druid who was once involved in protests against the excavation of a Bronze Age wooden henge found on a Norfolk beach. It was the henge dig that first brought Ruth to Norfolk, as part of a team led by her archaeology professor Erik Andersen. And there was, of course, a real henge found in Norfolk.

Right:
The path across the marshes.

Following pages:
Holme-next-the-Sea, where the real Seahenge was excavated.

In the spring of 1998, spikes of prehistoric timber appeared on the beach at Holme-next-the-Sea, on the north Norfolk coast. Wood expert Maisie Taylor was called to investigate and, on her second visit, she brought her husband, renowned archaeologist Francis Pryor, with her. In his brilliant book *Seahenge* Francis describes walking across the sand as the sun comes up and reveals a rough circle of oak posts, with what looks like an upside-down tree in the middle. He writes: 'I have rarely experienced anything so moving as the first time I saw the Holme circle.'

Francis knew immediately that the henge was either Neolithic or Bronze Age but he also knew that it would be possible to be more precise. This is because wood, unlike stone, can be dated to almost the exact year. Dendrochronology, or tree-ring dating, works on the principle that a tree lays down a growth ring every year: during wet years more and in dry years less. Dendrochronologists produce graphs, wonderfully named 'wiggle watching', showing a tree's growth over hundreds of years. But analysis of the timbers meant removing them, hence the protests from, amongst others, local druids.

As soon as I read the phrase 'local druids', I knew that such a character had to form part of my plot. Cathbad was born, first as a minor player and, later, as someone who would influence Ruth and Nelson in many ways and go on a redemptive journey of his own.

The Seahenge was endlessly fascinating to me. Archaeologists still can't say, with any certainty, why it was there or what its original function was. Were the roots of

Left:
'...the sand, rippling like a frozen sea, stretches far in front of her.' (*The Crossing Places*).

the upside-down tree used to hold sacrifices, even corpses? Maybe it represented Yggdrasil, the tree that, in Norse mythology, connects the nine worlds? Excavating the site proved particularly challenging, as the archaeologists battled with the tides and the shifting sands. I used this to dramatic effect in *The Crossing Places*.

The name Seahenge, originally given by the press, is misleading. The wooden circle would have been built on dry land. But the photograph of the timbers rising up out of the sand, with the sea in the background, has become the defining image of the henge. It even appears on the cover of Francis's book and, reluctantly, he had to accept the title too.

Having given Seahenge a central role, I was very nervous when I first met Francis Pryor at an event in Wisbech. I needn't have worried. Francis was very kind about the book and we have remained friends. Perhaps the biggest compliment Ruth has ever had came when Francis wrote his own murder mystery, *The Lifers' Club*. It features an archaeologist called Dr Ruth Galloway.

Francis is an incredibly inspiring speaker. In 2022, I did an event with him at the *Duke's Head* in King's Lynn. He described the importance of archaeology, how it is a record of ordinary people doing ordinary things: bakers making bread, potters kneeling by their kilns, prehistoric miners leaving fingerprints in the clay they wrapped round their antler picks to make them more secure. Archaeology isn't the study of kings and queens; it's about the wonders of the everyday.

Left:
Cley Marshes.

Spring is a magical time on the marshes of north Norfolk. Hundreds of millions of birds are on the move, heading north from southern Europe and Africa, and many will stop on the Norfolk wetlands to feed and build up fat reserves to fuel their onward journeys.

Cley* Marshes Visitor Centre, about forty miles east of Titchwell along the coast road, is the perfect place to observe these migrations. I was first invited to do an event there in 2019 and it was a moving experience to talk about the books with the ever-changing marshes behind me. In *The Lantern Men,* a cycle race is due to finish at the centre. Ruth waits there for Laura, Nelson's oldest daughter.

'It's even more humid when she arrives in Cley. She almost thinks that she can smell thunder in the air, hot and metallic. The visitor centre is a modern building that looks at home in the landscape, its curving lines following the hillside, grass growing on the roof. It's meant to be eco-friendly and has its own wind turbine, totally still today. Then she looks out over the marshes. There's a sign in front of her saying, "No Entry. Sensitive wildlife." Ruth thinks she knows how the wildlife feels.

The sky is now electric blue and the grass a strange luminous yellow. Here and there Ruth can see stretches of water, the same unearthly blue as the sky.'

*There's some debate about how to pronounce 'Cley' and even locals differ. I take my lead from Cley Spy, a shop that sells telescopes and birding guides.

Cley Marshes and Windmill.

Opposite and above:
'Sometimes...you see great flocks of wild geese
wheeling across the sky...' (*The Crossing Places*).

Early spring is also the time to see the snowdrops in the grounds of Walsingham Abbey. Walsingham has been a place of pilgrimage since the eleventh century, when a woman called Richeldis de Faverches had a vision of the Virgin Mary, who told her, in the bossy way such apparitions possess, to build a church. The original wooden 'holy house', said to replicate the house of the Holy Family in Nazareth, has long since disappeared, but a priory was built nearby by 1153. Many kings made pilgrimages to Walsingham. Henry VIII prayed for a son there but, in 1536, gave orders for it to be destroyed as part of the Dissolution of the Monasteries. Now a single arch is almost all that remains of the original priory but the village is still a major pilgrimage site. There's an Anglican shrine in Walsingham itself and, a mile away across the fields, stands the Catholic Slipper Chapel, so-called because the original pilgrims used to leave their shoes there before continuing barefoot. There's also a beautiful Russian Orthodox chapel in a converted railway carriage.

Above:
The Russian Orthodox Chapel in Walsingham.

Right:
The snowdrops in the Abbey grounds are famous.

Opposite and above:
The ruined priory at Walsingham.

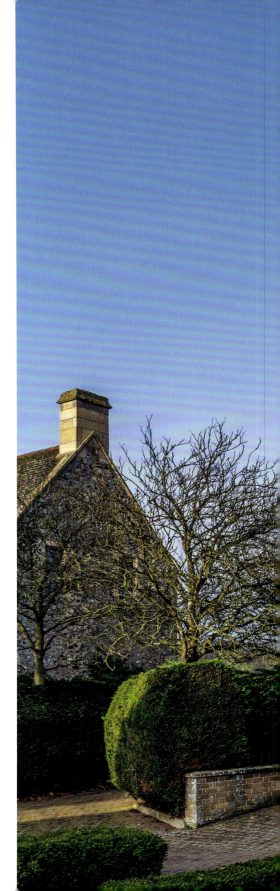

In 2015 I went on a pilgrimage to Walsingham to research *The Woman In Blue,* the eighth book in the series. I was honest with the priest in charge, Father Kevin, about my reasons for joining the party. He was very welcoming and generous in sharing his knowledge of the place. Even so, I found the trip a curiously unsettling experience. Processing through the village with lighted torches, it was impossible not to feel something sectarian and threatening in the air. Yet lighting a candle in the Slipper Chapel was a profoundly spiritual moment.

Visiting the snowdrops in February is a more pantheistic pilgrimage, yet not without its awe and wonder, as Ruth observes in *The Woman in Blue.*

'Ruth hadn't been expecting much from the snowdrops but, when she and Hilary walk through the gates, she actually catches her breath in wonder. Nothing much is left of the priory at Walsingham, just the archway and a few free-standing walls. But stretched out between them is a carpet of white. As if the church has risen up again in all her finery. Trees rise up like organ pipes and, far above them, a skylark is singing.'

Right:
The Slipper Chapel, near Walsingham. Pilgrims would leave their shoes here and walk the last mile barefoot. The official name is the Basilica of Our Lady of Walsingham.

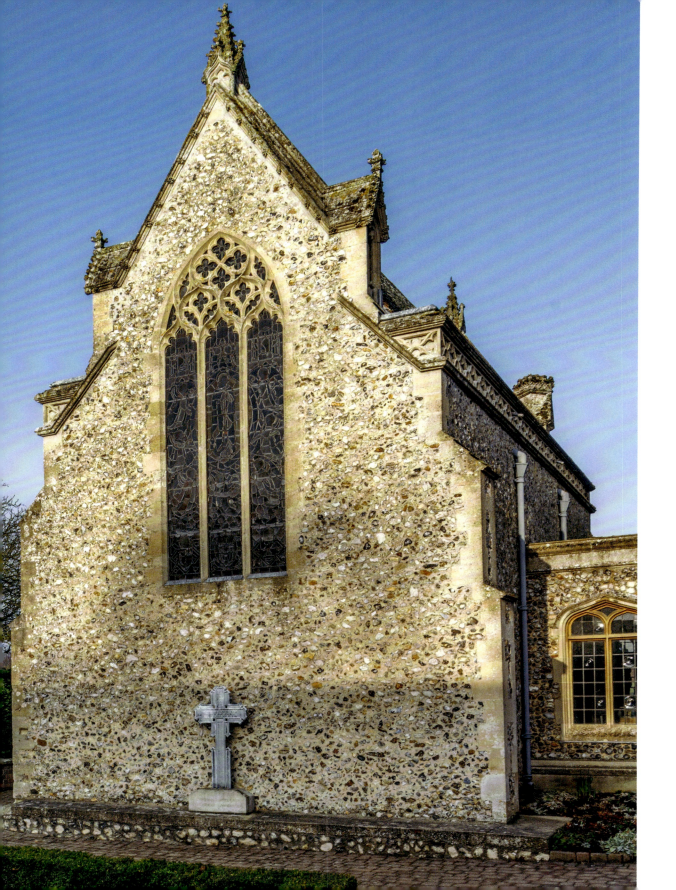

Many of my books seem to start in February. In *The Stone Circle*, I was able to use the deliciously spooky legend of Jack Valentine. It was Lee Mason, owner of Beccles Books, who told me about this tradition. On the morning of February 14th, there are three knocks on the door. You go to answer it but there's nobody there, just a parcel wrapped in brown paper. It's usually a present but there's a more sinister version called Snatch Valentine where the parcel has a string attached. The child tries to grab the present but the string pulls it just out of a reach. The child follows and, in some versions, is never seen again.

Perhaps the strangest spring I have ever described is the spring of 2020. *The Night Hawks*, the thirteenth book in the series, was written in 2020 but set in 2019, ending in December. I knew that, with the next book, I would have to face the question of whether or not to include lockdown. Should I pretend that Covid-19 had never happened and let Ruth and Nelson get on with their everyday, albeit complicated lives? Should I set the novel in the future? Surely Covid would be over by, say, 2022? Should I cram all the events into January and February and leave the virus as a dark cloud on the horizon?

In the end I decided to cover lockdown and the pandemic. The Spanish Flu epidemic of 1918 is thought to have killed over 50 million people worldwide. Yet, while the First World War provides the background for countless novels, the pandemic features in very few contemporary fictional accounts. I thought it would be a shame if the same thing happened with Covid. Having written a book about Ruth every year for fourteen years, it somehow seemed wrong to miss out 2020. Some real-life events, like Brexit and Donald Trump becoming US President, had already infiltrated Ruth's world. I thought that, looking back at the series, I would regret not mentioning the most devastating world health crisis of my lifetime. Also I thought that readers might want to know what happened to the characters in lockdown, and would wonder how they reacted. At the start of *The Locked Room*, Nelson is scoffing at the thought of hand sanitiser and Cathbad is putting a circle of protection around his cottage.

Spring tulips on the fens.

That all sounds very high-minded, but I have to admit that an evil, writerly part of my mind thought: what a great opportunity. All crime writers are obsessed with locked-room mysteries, so-called impossible murders where a body is found in a completely inaccessible place. In this book, Nelson is investigating a series of apparent suicides, including one in a room locked from the inside. But, when lockdown started in March 2020, the whole country became one big locked room. I wanted to explore this shared experience and also to highlight the plight of people for whom home was not a safe place. *The Locked Room* has some light-hearted moments – for example, Ruth's lockdown shopping list starts 'Cat Food, Wine' – but there is darkness too.

Spring 2020 was particularly beautiful or maybe we just appreciated it more. There were endless sunny days. The skies were cloudless and unpolluted by airplanes. I live just outside Brighton, on the south coast, and every day I took my one walk, as allowed by government regulations, in the direction of the sea. Like Ruth, I felt very lucky to have the luxury of staring out towards the horizon. I have a writing shed in my garden and I wrote every day, happy to have a job to do and a fictional world to escape to.

Much of *The Locked Room* takes place in the centre of Norwich, in the evocatively named Tombland. Rather disappointingly, the word derives from an Anglo-Saxon word meaning 'empty space', and the area was once a market place. At the beginning of the book, council workers digging up a road find a human skeleton. This

Left:
Norwich.

Following pages:
Norwich. 'The houses...leaning over as if
to watch the streets below.' (*The Chalk Pit*).

is not an uncommon occurrence in Norwich, which is famous for having a church, most of them complete with graveyards, for every week of the year – and a pub for every day. Ruth examines the bones and thinks that they might be the remains of a plague victim. There were plague outbreaks in Norwich in the fourteenth, fifteenth and sixteenth centuries. People were sealed into their houses and watchers were appointed to make sure that no one broke the rules. They carried sticks to enforce social distancing. The parallels with Covid-19 were all too obvious.

It is thought that one of Norfolk's most famous daughters, Julian of Norwich, survived the plague outbreak of 1373. Julian was an anchoress, a woman who lived in a cell attached to a church and devoted her life to prayer. Julian's book *Revelations of Divine Love,* written between the thirteenth and fourteenth centuries, is thought to be the earliest surviving book in the English language written by a woman. When I was writing *The Locked Room*, I found these lines from it very comforting.

> 'He said not "Thou shalt not be tempested, thou shalt not be travailed, thou shalt not be diseased", but he said, "Thou shalt not be overcome".'

Above:
The famously crooked Augustine Steward's House in the heart of Tombland.

Opposite
Houses in Norwich.

The Locked Room also includes one of Norfolk's most disturbing ghosts, the Grey Lady of Tombland. There are many origin stories about this apparition but the one I use in the book involves Augustine Steward's House, the famously crooked building in the heart of Tombland. Legend has it that, when the plague came to Norwich in 1578, the house was sealed up and, when it was opened again, there were three corpses inside, a young woman and her parents. The most gruesome part of the story is that the young woman had obviously tried to eat her parents to stay alive. Her ghost, dressed in a grey dress, is said to haunt the house and surrounding land.

This reminded me of a story told by my actor grandad. He was appearing at the Theatre Royal in Norwich and walking home through Tombland Alley late at night after a performance. A woman walked quickly past him, wearing a long grey cloak. She turned by the crooked house, as if to go in through a door, and disappeared. But, when Grandad passed the house, he saw that there was no door in the solid flint wall. What's more, he realized later, the hem of the woman's cloak had not disturbed the autumn leaves lying on the ground and her footsteps had made no sound. His landlady assured him that he'd seen the Grey Lady.

SUMMER

SUMMER

Looking back over the Ruth books, I was surprised at how many of them take place in the summer. In my mind, the literary weather is always grey and gloomy, with the occasional dramatic event, such as a snowstorm in *The House at Sea's End*, a flood in *The Ghost Fields* or even a gale in *A Room full of Bones*. But Norfolk is actually the driest and sunniest county in the UK. Hunstanton, on the north Norfolk coast, is known locally as 'Sunny Hunny', although my children, having trailed along the beach many times in the rain, laugh hollowly when I mention this.

In fifteen books, Ruth only has two proper summer holidays, to Blackpool in *Dying Fall* and to Italy in *The Dark Angel*. Andy and I took the kids to Blackpool to research *Dying Fall* and even rode the rollercoaster which plays an important part in the plot. It lasts for ten Hail Marys. Castello degli Angeli in *The Dark Angel* owes a lot to the hilltop town of Fontana Liri Superiore, where we have a family apartment.

Right:
The famous striped cliffs at Hunstanton.

Left and above:
Hunstanton.

Right:
The blue and yellow. The steam engine and tender are running on the Wells & Walsingham Light Railway.

Good weather does feature in the Norfolk books too. In *The Woman in Blue*, I set myself the challenge of writing a scary scene on a sunny afternoon, when Daisy walks home across the fields.

> 'She stops. Silence. Just a bird singing somewhere very high up. Blue sky, yellow flowers, like one of Victoria's paintings. Has her pursuer taken another path? Is she safe? Or have they stopped too? This last is somehow the most terrifying thought of all.'

The beautiful seaside town of Cromer makes guest appearances in a few of the books. Ruth and Shona visit the beach for a rather bad-tempered day out in *The Outcast Dead*. In *The Dark Angel* and *The Stone Circle,* Nelson meets an old colleague, who has retired to the town. This passage is from *The Dark Angel*.

> 'Nelson and Freddie Burnett are sitting on a bench, looking down on Cromer pier and esplanade. It's a sunny day and the beach is full of families building sandcastles, eating ice creams, venturing into the freezing North Sea. On the smooth lawn behind, a group of elderly men are playing bowls. It seems wrong to be talking about murder and arson...'

Incidentally, Cromer also makes an appearance in *Emma* by Jane Austen. Emma's father describes it as 'the best of all the sea-bathing places.'

Above and right:
Cromer – 'the best of all the sea-bathing places.'

Following pages:
Cromer pier.

Cromer pier.

Churches feature in many of the Ruth books. In the Middle Ages, Norfolk was a prosperous place, made wealthy by farming and the wool trade. The Domesday Book (a survey commissioned by William the Conqueror and completed in around 1086) notes that the county was one of the most densely populated places in the kingdom. Although this prosperity was already in decline when the Black Death exacerbated matters in 1349, one legacy is the preponderance of churches. Every tiny village seems to possess a handsome place of worship, often with towers or spires visible for miles in the flat landscape. Norfolk has more surviving medieval churches than any county in England.

Right:
Norwich Cathedral at night. The churches are beacons in the landscape.

Left:
Pull's Ferry, Norwich.

My first four novels were all set in Italy and featured battalions of angels and saints. My father, Felice, was Italian and his life was the inspiration for my first published book, *The Italian Quarter*. I'm very proud of my Italian heritage but I thought it was time for find some new subjects and settings. When I wrote my first crime novel, *The Crossing Places*, I said to myself: 'no Italians and no Catholics.' I stuck to the 'Italians' rule until *The Dark Angel* but there are Catholics everywhere. Nelson is a lapsed Catholic, as is Judy. Cathbad calls himself a druid and a shaman but still prays to the saints of his Irish Catholic boyhood. Ruth, raised by evangelical Christian parents, is a confirmed atheist. The following exchange between Nelson and DS Dave Clough comes from *The Janus Stone*, the second book in the Ruth series.

'"Nuns are creepy, though," says Clough.

"My aunt's a nun," says Nelson, to shut him up. In fact, Sister Margaret Mary of the Sacred Heart is his great-aunt, his grandmother's sister. He hasn't seen her for years.

"You're joking! You're a Catholic then?"

"Yes," says Nelson, though he hasn't been to church since Rebecca's first holy communion, eight years ago.

"Bloody hell, boss. I wouldn't have had you down as religious."

"I'm not," says Nelson. "You don't have to be religious to be a Catholic."'

Norwich Cathedral looms over *The Locked Room*.
Nelson imagines his mother saying, 'It was ours once',
a remark Catholics cannot help making when visiting
a pre-Reformation church. Whilst researching *A Room
Full of Bones*, the fourth book in the series, I was shown
round the cathedral by a very knowledgeable guide. I had
already decided that the book would include Julian of
Norwich whose statue, alongside Saint Benedict, guards
the entrance to the building. In my head, Julian had a cat,
a ginger tom like Ruth's Flint. Imagine my surprise when I
came face-to-face with the stained-glass window showing
Mother Julian – and her distinctly orange cat.

This is Ruth's reaction.

'Ruth looks, and sees in the coloured glass a woman
in a nun's habit, covered by a rather grand cloak. But
what makes her look twice is the creature at Julian's
feet.

"It's a cat!" she says in delight.'

Above and right:
The cloisters, Norwich Cathedral.

Brancaster.

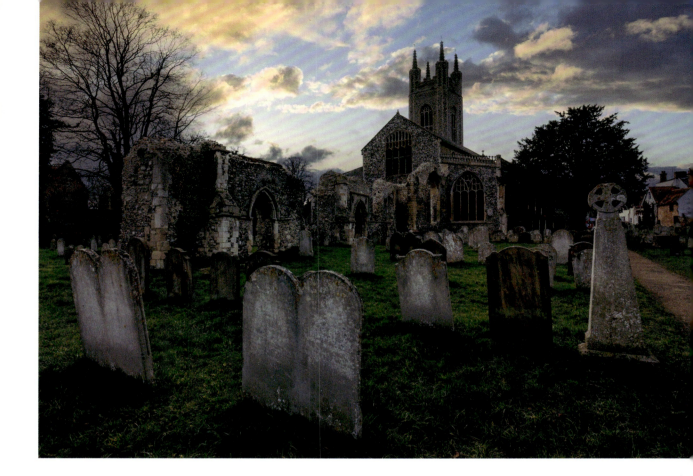

Above:
St Mary's, Bungay, where Black Shuck is said to have been seen in the graveyard.

Opposite:
The ruined church at Saxlingham Thorpe, which features in *The Outcast Dead*.

In *The Outcast Dead*, Ruth, her American friend, Frank, and her daughter, Kate, visit the ruined church at Saxlingham Thorpe. *The Dark Angel* mentions the legendary visit, to St Mary's in Bungay, North Suffolk, of the Devil in the form of a black dog. In *The Last Remains*, Kate and Ruth search for Cathbad in the deconsecrated church of St Mary's, Houghton-on-the-Hill.

St Mary's has a fascinating history. In 1992 a man called Bob Davey discovered a ruin near a deserted bridleway in the Breckland district of Norfolk. It was hardly recognizable as a building – just an ivy-covered shape in a field. When Bob investigated, he found the shell of a church, with no ceiling and crumbling walls. Bob began a one-man mission to save St Mary's. The difficulties seemed insurmountable. For a start, the building was being used by Satanists, and Bob had to muster friends from the Territorial Army to frighten them off. The indefatigable

St Mary's, Bungay.

Bob, together with a group of volunteers, cut back the ivy and raised the money to reroof the nave and chancel. They cleared the interior and laid a new floor. Then a contractor spotted paint underneath the limewash on one of the walls. Even Bob could not believe what was revealed. There were six layers of paint but the oldest dated back to the eleventh century, priceless artwork showing the creation of Eve, the Last Judgement and the raising of the dead. The paint had faded to a wonderful gold but there were traces of vermillion, one of the earliest known instances of this colour seen in the UK. On the south wall, a man in a red hat could be seen turning the spokes of a giant wheel.

Bob Davey died in 2020. Covid restrictions meant that his many friends and supporters could not attend the funeral. But his hat was placed on a tree stump by the door of his beloved church. It's there to this day.

I'm very grateful to Alan Brinsdon, one of the volunteer caretakers, for showing me round the church. It's a beautiful, peaceful place and, though the village that surrounded it has disappeared, you can feel the benign presence of the long-dead parishioners.

Right:
St Mary's, Houghton-on-the-Hill, a church raised from the dead.

St Mary's, Houghton-on-the-Hill.

Bob is definitely the inspiration for the mysterious figure who greets Ruth and Kate at St Mary's in *The Last Remains*.

> "'That's the wheel of fortune,'" says a voice from the doorway.
>
> Mother and daughter wheel round and Ruth knows that they were both expecting Cathbad, though the voice isn't like his. It's deeper with a trace of a Norfolk accent.
>
> A small man with a beard is addressing them. "Who controls the wheel of fate? One minute we are raised up, the next we are in the depths.'"

Later Ruth wonders if the man was a Church Grim, a guardian spirit who, in Nordic folklore, is said to protect the welfare of a particular church. There's no doubt who was the protector of St Mary's, Houghton-on-the-Hill.

Right:
Overstrand.

I knew that the second Ruth book, *The Janus Stone*, would take place in summer and would culminate in a – very slow – chase on the Norfolk Broads. To research this I needed the help of my Aunt Marge.

A quick note on my rather complicated maternal family. My grandfather, Frederick Goodwin, was a Variety entertainer and is the inspiration for my Brighton Mysteries, set in the theatrical world of the 1950s and 60s. Frederick fought in the First World War, in the trenches and in the newly formed Royal Flying Corps. When the war ended, he was an acting Major in the RFC, aged only twenty-one. He never talked about his war-time service, but he did once say, to my mum: 'After everything I'd seen in the war, there was only one job I could do – become a comedian.' So he did. He changed his name to Dennis Lawes and began a peripatetic life on the Variety Circuit. Along the way he married my grandmother, Ellen Griffiths and they had a daughter, my mother, Sheila. Ellen and Dennis divorced when mum was about four and, very unusually for the times, Dennis kept custody of his daughter. Her life, like his, was one of touring, theatrical boarding houses and myriad theatres. My mother was an extraordinary woman, resilient, positive and life-affirming. She is the model for Justice Jones in my children's series.

Left:
The Norfolk Broads.

Ellen also married again, to a musician called Walter (Wally) Taylor. They had one daughter, my Aunt Marjorie. Marge didn't meet her older sister until she was ten, and she remembers being dazzled by the beautiful stranger who walked into her house. Despite the ten-year age difference, the two sisters became good friends. Marge had two children, Jane and Ben. Jane and I were close in age and grew up together. Jane died of breast cancer in 2014. I still miss her.

Dennis then married Sonya, a dancer and Vivien Leigh lookalike, and they had a son, Roger. His third wife was another dancer, Sylvia, and they had a daughter, Corinne. Because Grandad's wives got progressively younger, Corinne and I are of a similar age and she is significantly younger than her nieces, my older sisters, Giulia and Sheila. Corinne has two daughters, Katie and Ellie. It seems amazing that Katie and Ellie, still in their early thirties, had a grandfather who fought in the First World War.

Right:
Hickling, Norfolk Broads.

For most of her life, Marge has lived in Norfolk. She has been a great help with all the books, always happy to explore new locations and contribute a few local legends (the gorier the better). Marge is also a keen sailor and has a boat moored at Reedham in the area known as the Broadland District. *Ashmore* is an ex-hire boat, the sort known as a 'bath-tub'. She has a pointed nose with railings all round (I am sketchy at nautical terminology). At the back, comfortable seats are lined with striped cushions made by Marge. Below is a small cabin with a kitchen and a sofa that pulls out to make a double bed. I have many happy memories of that boat, especially when Jane and I took our young families for days out, taking turns at the helm, having picnics on the river bank with wine in the Thermos flask.

Reedham was a very jolly mooring. Marge and the other boat owners seemed to spend their on-shore time having a continual round of parties, from summer barbecues to mulled wine gatherings at Christmas, with lights rigged up along the pontoons. But, like any crossing place, it has its own magic, as I describe in *The Janus Stone*.

'Ruth sees the river flowing past them, smooth as silk. Fields rise on either side, the corn as tall as they are. It is getting dark and the birds are flying low over the reeds. Ahead of them the river divides into two, like an illustration in a storybook. Which path will you take?'

Left:
Horsey Mere, which features in
The Janus Stone.

In *The Janus Stone*, a dangerously unstable octogenarian has kidnapped Ruth and is heading for Horsey Mere on the North Rivers. To get there he has to pass under Potter Heigham Bridge, which is notoriously low. Marge suggested that we made the journey in an electric boat, rather than risk *Ashmore*.

> "'And an electric boat is good for a murder,' said Marge.*
> "Why?"
> "Because it's silent.'"

Marge and I, accompanied by Alex, Juliet and Andy, climbed into the flimsy-looking boat, which looked more like a child's toy than anything water-worthy. We followed the post markers (red on the right towards the sea, green on the left) and passed under the bridge. The river opens out with terrifying suddenness, into Candle Dyke and the Mere. It's like the Elizabeth Jane Howard ghost story, *Three Miles Up*, where, after taking up a mysterious stranger called Sharon, two men on a boating holiday find themselves floating in a no-man's-land without shores or horizons.

*Marge has a distinctly criminal mind and is very good at thinking up plots. She is the inspiration for Peggy Smith, the murder consultant, in *The Postscript Murders*.

Potter Heigham Bridge.
The bridge plays a crucial part in
the plot of *The Janus Stone*.

Another unforgettable summer trip was in 2022. *The Last Remains* features the incredible Neolithic flint mines at Thetford in Norfolk with the evocative name of Grime's Graves. I mentioned that I was researching the book whilst giving a talk in Swaffham. Afterwards, a charming lady offered to put me in touch with a fellow dog walker, Tim Lynch, who worked at the site. I contacted Tim and he kindly agreed to give me and Andy a personal tour of the mines.

It was during a spell of very hot weather. When we turned off the road, the fields were parched and yellow. Aerial views of Grime's Graves show that the grass is pockmarked, like the surface of the moon, with hundreds of indentations, each one marking the presence of a mine shaft. You can't see these craters very well from ground level, so it can seem as if you are walking through empty countryside. Far from it, you are walking across one of the archaeological marvels of the world. Here's a description from *The Last Remains*.

'Ruth, driving through the gates, can see nothing but a long road, with trees on either side. She remembers the site being a huge field, although it is surrounded by Thetford Forest. But, suddenly, the sky opens up and she's driving through a wide space of sun-bleached grass. It reminds her of the ghost fields, the abandoned airbases scattered throughout Norfolk, now mostly converted into farms but retaining some of the vastness and menace of their original use.'

Left:
Grime's Graves. Descending into the mine
was an unforgettable experience.

I was rather alarmed when Tim gave us hard hats and safety harnesses. They weren't needed for the first mine shaft, which is the one used when school parties visit the site. You climb backwards down the ladder – 'going back into the past' said Tim – and find yourself in a circular space with chalk walls rising seven metres above you, studded with jet-like flints. It is incredible to think that the original miners excavated the shafts using only antler picks and animal bones, like scapulae. They dug out the flint and broke it into smaller nodules which were hauled to the surface in wicker baskets. You can still see the rope marks above the entry to one of the galleries, or tunnels. The shaft was then filled in with rubble. Nothing was wasted.

It's not known whether the miners had lights or worked through touch. According to Tim, one theory was that sunlight would be reflected on the white chalk piled at the foot of the shaft. We climbed back up ('forwards into the future') and then descended into a deeper shaft, not open to the public. Here we crawled along tunnels used by the Neolithic excavators. We saw the bones of dead animals, a huge rock in the shape of a human torso and – incredibly – fingerprints preserved on an antler pick. I took a picture of Andy crawling through one of the smallest tunnels. I was in front and had just reached a place where I could sit upright. Andy looked up and smiled. I've never seen him looking so happy.

Thetford.

Left and above:
Thetford Forest.

AUTUMN

AUTUMN

Autumn is a spectacular season in Norfolk. The migrant birds arrive, wheeling across the vast skies, to spend the winter on the marshes, estuaries and mudflats. It is estimated that, every year, over 100,000 wading birds – lapwing, plover, pink-footed geese – travel to Breydon Water, near Great Yarmouth in east Norfolk, to feed on nutritious invertebrates. At twilight, the air is filled with murmuration, starlings like iron filings in the sky, constantly changing and regrouping. Cathbad would say that, at dawn and dusk, the membrane between this world and the next is very thin. Certainly, the light is ethereal, the low sun turning the reed beds ablaze, the shallow water an unearthly blue.

In *The Crossing Places,* Ruth's neighbour David tells her:

> "'In the winter, the Saltmarsh can be covered in birds, all trying to find something to eat on the mudflats. Sometimes there are as many as two thousand pink-footed geese, for example, coming from Iceland and Greenland and there are lots of native waterfowl too: goldeye, gadwell, goosander, shoveller, pintail. I've even seen a red-backed shrike…'"

Birds wing their way through all the Ruth books. In
A Room Full of Bones, Nelson hears the word 'murmuration'
in a fever dream. In *The Lantern Men*, Ruth follows a
strange, glowing owl. In *The Locked Room* she befriends
a crow she calls Corbyn. In *The Ghost Fields*, geese fly
overhead, an echo of the lost war planes. Everything,
Cathbad tells Ruth in *Dying Fall*, is a sign of something.

Above:
Murmuration, Snettisham.

In *The Lantern Men*, Ruth hears about the legend of the mysterious cloaked figures who haunt lonely marshland, carrying flickering lanterns. On dark nights, the light looks welcoming, but you must never follow it because it will lead you to certain death.

Legend has it that this is what happened to Joseph Bexfield, a wherryman, working on the Norfolk Broads. One summer evening in August 1809, Joseph moored his wherry – a traditional cargo boat with sails – at Thurlton Staithe on the River Yare and walked across the marshes to a pub called the *White Horse Inn*. Joseph was just settling down to a hot rum when he remembered that he'd left a package behind on his boat. What was worse was that it was something that his wife has asked him to buy in Norwich. He would have to go back and fetch it.

'Don't go, Joe,' begged the other boatmen. 'It's dark and the Lantern Men are about.'

But Joseph must have been a loving husband, or afraid of his wife, because he insisted on retracing his steps back to the mooring. His body was found floating downstream the next day. The boatmen knew what had happened. Joseph had met the Lantern Men.

Left:
A traditional Norfolk wherry at Thurne.

Right:
Beware of mysterious lights
on the marsh at night.

As I discovered, there are many myths and legends
about mysterious lights appearing on marshland at night.
One version links them to a wicked blacksmith called Jack
who tricks the Devil and so escapes Hell but can never be
allowed into Heaven. Jack is condemned to walk the earth
for ever, carrying a single coal from Hell inside a pumpkin.
The tradition of putting lighted candles into pumpkins at
Halloween, also known as jack-o'-lanterns, probably comes
from this fable.

Jack is not the only creature abroad at night. Sometimes
the blacksmith is called Will and, in English folklore,
marsh lights are often called will-o'-the-wisps, wisp
meaning a bundle of twigs tied together to make a torch.
There are some regional variations, hobby lanterns in
the north and pixie lights in Devon and Cornwall, where
hapless travellers are said to be 'pixie-led'.

These legends exist all around the world. In Scandinavia
the lights are said to be the souls of unbaptised children.
In America they are 'spook lights' or 'ghost lights'. In
Louisiana, a *feu follet* (from the French for fool's fire)
is a soul sent back from the dead, usually hell-bent on
vengeance. In South America they are called *luz mala*,
evil lights, or *la candileja*. *Chir batti* (ghost lights) is the
name given to strange dancing lights seen on the Banni
grasslands in India. In Australia, *Min Min lights* are often
reported glowing in the Outback.

All these tales have one message in common: do not
follow these spooky, ghostly, foolish lights. If you do, if you
leave the path, then yours will be the fate of poor Joseph

Left:
Mudflats at Snettisham.

Bexfield. It's true that in some legends (*luces del dinero* in Mexico, for example) the lights are said to lead to buried treasure. But would you trust any riches found in this way? Especially when, as in the Irish version, you are required to take a dead man's hand with you to help in your quest.

There is, of course, a scientific explanation for this phenomenon. Dead matter trapped in the mud releases methane which mixes with phosphines to create a blue light, or phosphorescence. One winter evening, my publicist Hannah and I were driving to an event at Cley Marshes Visitor Centre (which features in several of the books). We were both shocked when a glowing white bird flew in front of the car, its feathers almost incandescent in the moonlight. At the visitor centre, Dr Duncan Macdonald, senior partner at WildSounds & Books, told us that birds sometimes eat phosphorescent plants which cause them to glow in the dark. From this comes another wonderful Norfolk legend, that of the glowing owls. These luminous creatures can either be a portent of death or of good fortune. You take your pick. Hannah and I decided on the latter.

So, if you set out to explore Norfolk, keep to the tracks and don't take any unnecessary risks. And, if you visit Thurlton Staithe on the Broads, you can see the grave of Joseph Bexfield, the loving husband, or was he the man who was more afraid of his wife then he was of the Lantern Men?

Left:
St Benet's Abbey.

Autumn is also the season of mists. Fog is the crime writer's friend. You can hide murderers and clues alike and there's nothing as sinister as a landscape that suddenly becomes featureless and alien. This is the scene when Ruth arrives at the fictional Black Dog Farm, near Sheringham, in *The Night Hawks*.

> 'The house appears windows first, like the Cheshire Cat's grin. She sees dark frames, sinister in their very symmetry, then the door, then the roof with the weathercock, invisible today but creaking gently. The mist blows around the farm buildings like smoke.'

The name Black Dog Farm refers to a famous Norfolk legend, that of Black Shuck*, a spectral hound whose appearance is an omen of the very worst kind. The word 'shuck' derives from the Old English word 'scucca' meaning devil or fiend. The dog is usually described as coal black with red eyes. You can, apparently, see his claw marks on the door of St Mary's church in Bungay. There are many such legends around the country, including the Northern Gytrash, who even gets a mention in *Jane Eyre*.

*In Norfolk Black Shuck does not have an article. For clarity's sake, I have used the definite article in the book, to some people's considerable annoyance.

W A Dutt, in his 1901 *Highways & Byways in East Anglia,* describes the creature thus:

> 'He takes the form of a huge black dog, and prowls along dark lanes and lonesome field footpaths, where, although his howling makes the hearer's blood run cold, his footfalls make no sound. You may know him at once, should you see him, by his fiery eye; he has but one, and that, like Cyclops', is in the middle of his head. But such an encounter might bring you the worst of luck: it is even said that to meet him is to be warned that your death will occur before the end of the year. So you will do well to shut your eyes if you hear him howling; shut them even if you are uncertain whether it is the dog fiend or the voice of the wind you hear. Should you never set eyes on our Norfolk Snarleyow you may perhaps doubt his existence, and, like other learned folks, tell us that his story is nothing but the old Scandinavian myth of the black hound of Odin, brought to us by the Vikings, who long ago settled down on the Norfolk coast.'

Right:
Fog is the crime writer's friend.

Following pages:
Where the earth meets the sky.

Autumn mist at Holme.

The Night Hawks is set in 2019 but was actually written during the lockdown of 2020. It's the only time that I have written a book without visiting Norfolk. Perhaps as a reaction to this, the books is full of local myths and legends. As well as Black Shuck, there's the Sheringham Mermaid and the Norfolk Sea Serpent.

Above:
Sheringham, where the mermaid came ashore...

The Sheringham Mermaid supposedly emerged from the sea, drawn by the music of the church choir. Her likeness is carved into one of the pews of All Saints, an ancient church in Upper Sheringham. The last sighting of the sea serpent was in Eccles-on-Sea in 1936. The creature was spotted by three august personages who sound like the beginning of a joke. The former Mayor of Norwich, a Labour MP and a prominent trade unionist were going for a companionable stroll when they saw something skimming along the water.

'I am positive,' said Mr Witard, the ex-Mayor, 'that what we saw was a sea serpent. We were all on the beach together on Wednesday evening when we saw the creature and it was a perfectly clear evening... this creature looked like a huge snake. Its action in swimming was wormlike and not the roll of a porpoise. Its speed was terrific. I said not less than a mile a minute in my letter, but 90 to 100 miles an hour is not an exaggerated estimate. I have by me a copy of the *Strand* magazine for 1895 containing an article on sea serpents. One of the serpents described is exactly like the one I saw.'
(From the *Eastern Daily Press* archives, described in an article published in 2017.)

Left:
Fishing boats at Sheringham.

Blakeney – the name means Black Island – is a beautiful part of the north Norfolk coast. In *The Night Hawks*, Ruth walks from Cley to Blakeney Point, a spit of land that juts out into the sea.

> 'They walk along the beach, scrubby shingle on one side and the sea on the other. Occasionally Ruth sees sea poppies and clumps of samphire. A yacht goes by, its sails very white against the blue. In the distance is a curious blue house like an upturned boat…there are patches of still water here and, as they pass, the birds rise up in clouds.'

Blakeney is also famous for its seals. Blakeney Point Nature Reserve is home to England's largest seal colony with over four thousand pups born every year. Pupping season is from October to January. The best way to see the seals is from the water. My cousin Jane and I took our children out in the seal boats many times, while Marge and my mum ate Eccles cakes in a caravan-turned-café on the seashore. Ruth and Kate make the trip in *The Night Hawks*.

Above left:
Seals at Blakeney Point.

Above:
The old lifeboat house, now an
information centre.

Following pages:
'Thunder is rolling above them...Cathbad turns
to him, grinning..."Cosmic energy", he says.
Nelson ignores him.'

'In the distance Ruth can see...the islands of sand and seagrass, linked by lagoons of blue water, the birds rising into the air at their approach. It's a beautiful landscape, but a slightly eerie one, home to countless sea creatures, somehow inhospitable to humans.

"Seals," says Troy. "Over there."

Ruth realises that the grey rocks at the water's edge are, in fact, seals, sunning themselves on the sand...'

Above and above right:
Blakeney. When we first meet Cathbad,
he is living in a caravan in the village.

In *The Crossing Places,* Cathbad is living in a caravan near the beach in Blakeney. This is our first encounter with the lab assistant and part-time druid.

'Inside, the first sensation is of being in a tent. Midnight blue draperies hang from the ceiling and cover every piece of furniture. Ruth can just make out a bunk bed with cupboards under it, a cooker, covered with rust and food stains, a wooden bench seat and a table, this time covered with billowing red material. The blue drapes give a strangely dreamlike feeling, as do the twenty or so dream-catchers twinkling from the ceiling. The air is thick and musty...

Cathbad gestures them towards the bench before seating himself in a high wizard's chair. First point to him, thinks Ruth.

"Mr Malone," says Nelson. "We're investigating a murder and we'd like to ask you a few questions."

Cathbad looks at them calmly. "You're very abrupt," he says. "Are you a Scorpio?"

Cathbad is right about this, at least.'

The beach at Wells-next-the-Sea.
'Everything is golden and blue...The beach huts are outlined against the pine trees like a postcard from another age.' (*The Last Remains*).

Right:
Jarrold, Norwich. This family-owned store
has supported the Ruth books from the
very beginning.

The nights are drawing in and the ninth Ruth book, *The Chalk Pit,* takes place mostly in darkness, in the tunnels below Norwich. I first had the idea for this book when I was doing a book signing in Jarrold, the wonderful family-owned department store in the centre of the city. After the event, Marketing Manager Carole Slaughter mentioned that there was an undercroft, or cellar, below the store. 'Would you like to see it?'

Carole took out a huge key and led the way though departments full of clothes and soft furnishings. My friend, the writer Elizabeth Haynes, had been at the event and she came too. Carole opened a low door and we were in a different world: low, vaulted ceiling, chalk walls, a sense of echoing chambers.

'How far does it go back?' I asked.

'Not far,' said Carole, 'but there are tunnels all over the town. Some people say you can walk the length of Norwich underground.'

I wanted to find out more and soon heard about the famous incident in 1988 when a double-decker bus fell into a sinkhole on the Earlham Road. The chasm had appeared when a medieval chalk-mining tunnel had unexpectedly opened up. These tunnels, which form a subterranean network below the city, occasionally link up with crypts and undercrofts from Norwich's many churches. I started to investigate urban myths of communities living underground: the Tunnel People in Las Vegas, the Empire of the Dead in Paris, the Rat Tribe of Beijing.

In *The Chalk Pit*, Ruth finds a body in a tunnel under the Guildhall, the beautiful chequerboard building in the centre of Norwich that has, in the past, been a toll house, a court and a prison.

'The tunnel leads downwards, and the plastered walls give way to chalk, the floor moving quickly from brick to rubble that crunches underfoot. Ted's torch picks out a well-crafted roof, lined with brick and flint.

"Probably an old chalk mine," he says.

Ruth puts her hand on the wall. It's unpleasantly moist to the touch, as if it's sweating.

"There's a tunnel from the castle to the Guildhall," says Ruth.'

Opposite:
Norwich Cathedral. Many churches in Norfolk have crypts or undercrofts.

Above:
Hidden street under Castle Meadow in Norwich.

Following pages:
The Guildhall in Norwich. Ruth finds human bones here in *The Chalk Pit*.

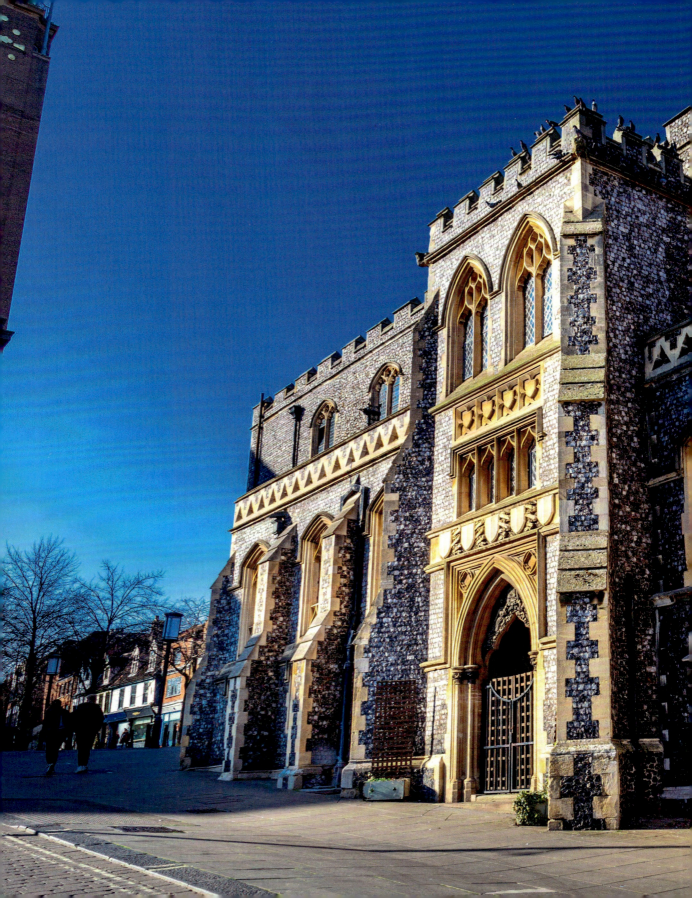

Carole and the team at Jarrold have always been very good to me. I had only published one Ruth book when I was invited to one of their famous literary lunches at Norwich City Football Club (catering by the great Delia Smith). The other guests were Matthew Hall and Wilbur Smith. Both were very kind to the new kid on the Norfolk block. Chris Rushby, bookshop manager and the possessor of one of the best voices ever, took it upon himself to promote my books in the store. There was even a sign saying 'Elly Griffiths, Queen of Norfolk Crime.' Chris's successor, Holly Ainley, was equally supportive and presided over several memorable launches, including an online event during lockdown. The current bookshop manager, Rebekka Edmond-Humphreys, has just organized a fantastic evening for the fifteenth and last (for now) Ruth Galloway mystery.

FOR SALE

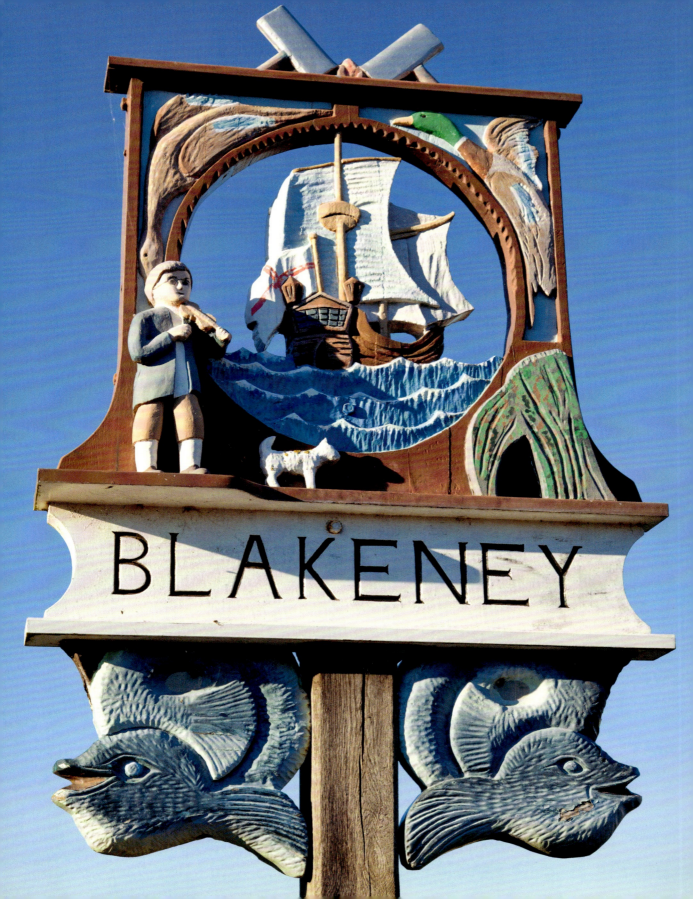

BLAKENEY

As a small thank you, I wrote a special short story as part of the celebrations for the store's 250th anniversary in 2020. Called *The Man in Black*, it starts in the book department.

> 'Ruth loves the bookshop at Jarrold. Just a few steps down from the worldly pleasures of perfume and make-up (she admires the packaging, all sharp corners and minty colours, but never knows how to apply it) and she is among friends. She moves in an almost trance-like state around the shelves. Although this is a department in a busy department store, it has a proper bookshop feel, a sense that you could get lost behind Local History and not be found for several days.'

The story is set around Halloween and concerns creatures from Norfolk legend called Hytersprites. They're usually described as malignant pixies, sometimes with fur and whiskers, who capture children and small animals. They live in the tunnels under Blakeney, said to run from the Guildhall to the Friary.

The village signpost for Blakeney references another local legend. It shows a bewigged violinist and his rather sad-looking cat. According to folklore, a violinist went into the Blakeney tunnel years ago, accompanied by his white cat. It was said that you could hear him playing underground and then, suddenly, the music stopped. The man and his cat were never seen again.

No cats are harmed in my story.

Opposite:
The signpost at Blakeney. Note the violinist and his cat.

Cows in the mist.
A three-legged calf appears on Ruth's doorstep in *The Janus Stone*.

WINTER

WINTER

I n December 2013 Norfolk was devastated by terrible floods. Fields turned into lakes and villages were cut off completely. Seals were seen swimming along the coast road. It was a natural disaster, but it was also the perfect setting for a murder mystery. In *The Ghost Fields,* Ruth is marooned at Blackstock Hall, near Hunstanton. When she looks out of the window, the landscape has changed completely.

'Water stretches as far as the eye can see. Occasionally trees and hedge-tops mark the boundaries of fields but otherwise everything is uniformly blue and sparkling. It's beautiful but it's also disconcerting, as if she has woken up to find herself in another world, a watery Narnia.'

Right:
Snow-covered beach.

Shipwrecks at Hunstanton.

Wiveton Hall.
The inspiration for Blackstock Hall in *The Ghost Fields*.

The title *The Ghost Fields* refers to abandoned airfields. At the end of the Second World War there were thirty-seven such military airbases in Norfolk. Only two – RAF Coltishall and RAF Marham – are still operational. The rest are derelict or have been adapted for agriculture, pigs rootling around in old hangars, administration offices turned to outhouses. Some still retain runways and control towers, occasionally with half-legible words painted on them: 'Bomb Group' or '8th in the East.' There are murals painted on some of the walls: regimental mascots, religious imagery, depictions of planes and airmen, some realistic, others oddly surreal and touching. The race is now on to preserve this artwork, painted by unknown artists on buildings not meant to last. Surviving examples can be found at places like Shipham, Flixton and Wendling – the names are wonderful too.

Above and right:
Abandoned airfield at Flixton.

The idea for *The Ghost Fields* came to me when I was driving past RAF Sculthorpe, near Fakenham. Once an airbase, now a heritage museum and training centre, the airfield looked sinister in the half-light. I was lost (not an unusual occurrence) so I stopped to get my bearings. I realized I was parked by a pub called *The Hour Glass*. What would it be like, I thought, to drink there, knowing that next day you might be flying to your death? The name of the pub would seem sinister in the extreme, the sands of life draining away. Rather disappointingly, I later discovered that, during the Second World War, the pub had been called *The Horse and Groom*. It began to acquire a rather unsavoury reputation, so the name was changed, whilst retaining the initials. But the seed of the story was sown.

Left:
'Nelson's not a fanciful man but...he imagines the sky full of lumbering Second World War planes, rising into the clouds and heading out to sea. He thinks of the men inside the control tower, listening to their briefing, not knowing whether they'll ever come back.' (*The Ghost Fields*).

Right:
'It looks wrong to see snow on a beach, like a negative, the black waves breaking on the white shore.' (The House at Sea's End).

The Ruth book that features the most wintery weather is probably the third in the series, *The House at Sea's End*, although the snowstorm actually occurs in the unseasonable month of April. Ruth and Nelson are snowed in at Sea's End House, situated in a thinly disguised Happisburgh, a village threatened by coastal erosion and, in places, slowly crumbling into the sea. Meanwhile, in one of the many similarly dangerous drives in the books, DS Judy Johnson battles through the snow to reach Ruth's cottage. Luckily Judy is a brilliant driver.

'New Road is a nightmare. One slip, Judy knows, and she'll plunge the car down the bank and will probably never be seen again....When she sees it, she thinks at first that she is hallucinating. A dark, hooded figure, trudging along at the side of the road. Who on earth would be walking along New Road through foot-high snow? Then she starts to panic. Her head spins with images of mysterious figures that appear beside unwary travellers, of car-crash victims who suddenly materialise on your back seat, grinning through their mangled faces, the third man – the hooded man – Christ on the road to Emmaus...'

The encounter is a fateful one for Judy.

Happisburgh is also the site of an incredibly important archaeological discovery. In 2013 a set of fossilized human footprints were found on the beach. They turned out to be 800,000 years old, the oldest human footprints outside Africa. Analysis suggests that about five individuals, adults and children, were walking upstream, along the edge of an estuary which became the River Thames. I wrote a short story about them. It's called *Turning Traitor,* which is part of my favourite quotation from my favourite author.

> 'Nothing in the world is hidden for ever…Sand turns traitor and betrays the footstep that passed over it.' Wilkie Collins, *No Name.*

Right:
Happisburgh Lighthouse.

Wells-next-the-Sea.
Cathbad and Judy buy a cottage here.

Turning Traitor starts with the family who left their marks in the sand.

‘At low tide the river is a wonderland, the mudflats are full of creatures that we can eat and the sand stretches for miles. Father says not to waste time, the tide can change very quickly and you can easily get stranded. But it's hard not to stop and look. The sand is cool under my feet and, if I rub with my big toe, it changes colour, becoming blue and grey with streaks of black. You can find shrimps there, grey-white with orange heads. If you're not quick enough, the sea birds will swoop down and take them from under your nose. Where the salt waves wash over, there are sand crabs, little creatures that burrow back down into the silt as soon as you see them. If you move fast enough, though, you can scoop them out of the sucking sand and they make good eating.'

Left:
The oldest human footprints outside Africa were found at Happisburgh in Norfolk.

Frosty morning, Salthouse.

The Night Hawks ends in December, just before Christmas. Nelson takes his dog, Bruno, for a walk, accompanied by his mother, Maureen. They go to Sandringham House and walk in the grounds.

> '"The Queen's here for Christmas," says Nelson. "You might see her."
>
> "Get along with you," says Maureen, but Nelson thinks she's keeping a pretty keen eye out all the same.'

Sandringham House is one of the many residences belonging to the British Royal Family. Sandringham, a village about seven miles north of King's Lynn, is recorded in the Domesday Book as 'sant-Dersingham', or the sandy part of Dersingham. After the Norman Conquest of 1066, the land was awarded to a Norman knight, although there is evidence of an older, Roman dwelling. In the Elizabethan era a large manor house was built on the site. It was replaced, in 1771, by a Georgian mansion. In 1862 the

Above:
Dersingham.

Opposite:
Sandringham, one of the many residences owned by the British Royal Family.

Left:
Sandringham House and grounds.
Nelson often walks Bruno here.

house and its estate of 8,000 acres was bought by Edward VII, Queen Victoria's eldest son, as a country retreat. Edward rebuilt the house in a style described by Pevsner as 'frenetic Jacobean.' Sandringham has been passed to each successive monarch and is now owned by King Charles III.

The late Queen Elizabeth II had a particular fondness for Sandringham, and for Norfolk. She often spent the winter months there and broadcast her first televised Christmas message from Sandringham in 1957. In 1977, to mark her Silver Jubilee, she opened the house and the grounds to the public for the first time. It is now possible to walk your dog in Sandringham Park, as Nelson does in several of the books.

Norfolk is particularly rich – in all senses – in stately homes. As you drive through the countryside, you frequently encounter high walls and impressive-looking gates. If you're lucky, a higher stretch of land will afford a glimpse of the house itself, four-square and symmetrical against a backdrop of trees. The fact that so much of the county is still in private hands is partly why the landscape is so well preserved, but it does sometimes feel as if many of its beauties are still behind closed doors.

Above and right:
Blickling Hall, where Anne Boleyn is said to have been born.

One of the most famous Norfolk mansions is Blickling Hall, where Anne Boleyn is said to have been born. The Hall contains a statue and portrait of Anne, Henry VIII's second wife, both of which bear the inscription, 'Anna Bolena hic nata 1507' (Anne Boleyn born here 1507). Her ghost, of course, walks.

Blickling Hall also contains an RAF museum, which features in *The Ghost Fields*. It seems a surprising thing to find in the grounds of a Jacobean manor house (built on the ruins of the original Tudor building) until you learn that RAF troops were stationed there in the Second World War. Much of the action in *The Ghost Fields* takes place in a fictional house called Blackstock Hall, which draws inspiration from Wiveton Hall, situated on the north Norfolk coast between Blakeney and Cley-next-the-Sea. Wiveton, built in 1652 on the site of an older building, is now famous as the setting for the TV documentary series *Normal for Norfolk*.

Blickling Hall.

Nelson and Clough visit Blackstock Hall when a body is found in an old warplane, excavated in a nearby field. Forensic tests show that the dead man was one of the Blackstock family.

'The drive...past flat fields criss-crossed with tiny streams; mournful-looking sheep stand marooned on grassy islands and geese fly overhead, honking sadly. The house is visible from miles away, a ship rising from a grey-green sea.

"I wouldn't like to live here," says Clough. "It's as bad as Ruth's place."

"It's a bit grander than Ruth's place."

Blackstock Hall is indeed grand, a stern brick-built edifice with a tower at each corner, but there is no comforting stately home feeling about it: no National Trust sign pointing to the tea rooms, no manicured lawns or Italian gardens. Instead the grass comes right up to the front door and sheep peer into the downstairs rooms. If there was a path to the front door, it vanished years, maybe centuries, ago.'

Frosty day on the Broads.

The only time I've ever written about Ruth at Christmas was in another short story, *Ruth's First Christmas Tree*. Ruth is determined to create the perfect Christmas for herself, two-year-old Kate and her new boyfriend, archaeologist Max Grey. So, for the first time in her life, she purchases a Christmas tree and decorates it. At this festive moment, Cathbad arrives with mulled wine and mince pies. As Ruth and Cathbad chat in the kitchen, Kate and Ruth's cat, Flint, destroys the tree.

I have occasionally invented things that have gone on to become true, Mother Julian's cat, for example. In this instance I was prophetic. In April 2022, we lost our beloved cat, Gus, aged 18. It was a long time before we could consider another pet but, in November, we adopted a kitten called Pip. Gus had always treated the Christmas tree with lofty distain, though he would pose beside it for tasteful pictures. Pip was *obsessed* with the tree, regularly launching himself into it and emerging covered in tinsel. When I look at the cover of *Ruth's First Christmas Tree*, which shows a broken bauble, I laugh hollowly.

There is a happy ending to the short story, which I won't spoil for you. There's also another scene where Ruth battles the elements to return to her beloved cottage.

'The snow is falling heavily now and her windscreen wipers struggle to keep even a patch of clear window. Ruth leans forward, hands tense on the wheel, peering into the night. Her headlights seem only to reflect more snow, the flakes whirling in a funnel of watery light...There's something mesmeric about the swirling snow; she imagines herself driving along this road for ever, Norfolk's answer to the Flying Dutchman, endlessly circling her destination, never again to reach the comforts of home. Only yesterday she bought one of those snow globes for Kate and had enjoyed seeing the child's face light up when the globe was agitated and the little plastic scene disappeared under the ensuing blizzard. Now it's as if she is trapped inside the glass toy, invisible behind the snowstorm.'

But Ruth gets home. And, for Ruth, home is always Norfolk.

A VIEW FROM BEHIND THE LENS

I'm a professional landscape photographer based in Suffolk in the heart of East Anglia and although my work takes me all over the country and to many parts of the world, I am best known for my atmospheric images of East Anglia.

Photography began as a hobby several years ago and as my passion for landscape photography grew I decided to focus on photographing my local area where I could spend more time behind the camera and less time behind the wheel. Close proximity and local knowledge meant I could respond to changing weather, learn quicker from my mistakes and build up both my portfolio and experience by returning to locations again and again.

Since those early days I have been fortunate to work on some fascinating projects with clients including the National Trust and English Heritage, and the resulting images have been widely published.

As an experienced photography tutor I have been running 1-2-1 and group workshops in East Anglia for over ten years, also leading photography workshops here for the National Trust, Forestry Commission and Royal Photographic Society. In recent years my range has increased to cover some of the beautiful areas around the UK – and further afield I lead photography tours to locations around the world… everywhere from Northumberland to Namibia.

The joy of landscape photography for me is the being there. Being a part of nature and witnessing its wonders. Those wonderfully unpredictable conditions and fleeting moments of light that make the heart beat a little faster. The thrill of watching the first light of the day creep over the

frozen stillness of a wintry landscape, while the air and my fingers tingle with the cold, and the challenge of capturing the atmosphere of moments like this is what it is all about.

Justin Minns

Left:
Sunset at Blakeney.

INDEX

First published in Great Britain in 2023 by

QUERCUS

Quercus Editions Ltd
Carmelite House
50 Victoria Embankment
London EC4Y 0DZ

An Hachette UK company

Copyright © 2023 Elly Griffiths

The moral right of Elly Griffiths to be
identified as the author of this work has been
asserted in accordance with the Copyright,
Designs and Patents Act, 1988.

All rights reserved. No part of this publication
may be reproduced or transmitted in any form
or by any means, electronic or mechanical,
including photocopy, recording, or any
information storage and retrieval system,
without permission in writing from the publisher.

A CIP catalogue record for this book is available
from the British Library

HB ISBN 978 1 5294 2752 3
EB ISBN 978 1 5294 2753 0

10 9 8 7 6 5 4 3 2 1

Designed by Paul Turner and Sue Pressley,
Stonecastle Graphics
Edited by Nick Freeth

Printed and bound in China.

Papers used by Quercus are from well-managed
forests and other responsible sources.

Picture Credits

All images © Justin Minns
with the exception of the following:

35 Edward Parker / Alamy Stock Photo
47 Ashley Cooper pics / Alamy Stock Photo
64 Sid Frisby / Alamy Stock Photo
112–113 Skyscan Photolibrary / Alamy Stock Photo
114–115 Martin Bache / Alamy Stock Photo
163 Kevin Snelling / Alamy Stock Photo
164–165 Nathaniel Noir / Alamy Stock Photo
168 eye35 stock / Alamy Stock Photo
180–181 David Burton / Alamy Stock Photo.

1. SANDRINGHAM

2. SLIPPER CHAPEL

3. W'SINGHAM ABBEY

4. WIVETON HALL

5. BLICKLING HALL

6. ST MARY'S CHURCH
BUNGAY

NORTH S

SEAHENGE

NORFOLK MARSHES

TITCHWELL MARSH

HUNSTANTON
OLD HUNSTANTON
HOLME-NEXT-THE-SEA

WELLS-NEXT-THE-SEA

BURNHAM MARKET

WALSINGHAM

SNETTISHAM
DERSINGHAM

1

2 3

FAKENHAM

KING'S LYNN

N O R

RAF MARHAM

N

DOWNHAM MARKET

HOUGHTON-ON-THE-HILL

N

THETFORD FOREST
GRIMES GRAVES

THETFORD

S U F F